DATE DUE

JAN 12	JAN 18 2001
JAN 29	FEB 2 2001
FEB 17	FEB 21 2001
MAR 06	MAR 07 2001
OCT 07	
NOV 05 1998	JAN 21 2002
DEC 02 1998	
JAN 29 1999	FEB 01 2002
FEB 24 1999	FEB 12 2002
JAN 21 2000	FEB 25 2003
FEB 04 2000	MAR 22 '04
FEB 21 2000	APR 20 '04
NOV 22 2000	NOV 6 '13
JAN 22 '04	
3/18/04	
APR 28 '04	

SPORTS GREAT
JOHN
ELWAY

Larry Fox

—Sports Great Books—

ENSLOW PUBLISHERS, INC.

44 Fadem Road
Box 699
Springfield, N.J. 07081
U.S.A.

P.O. Box 38
Aldershot
Hants GU12 6BP
U.K.

Library of Congress Cataloging-in-Publication Data:

Fox, Larry.
   Sports Great John Elway / by Larry Fox.
      p. cm. — (Sports great books)
      Summary: Follows the life of Denver Broncos star quarterback John Elway and his accomplishments on the pro football gridiron.
      ISBN 0-89490-282-2
      1. Elway, John, 1960-   — Juvenile literature. 2. Football players — United States — Biography — Juvenile literature. 3. Quarterback (Football) — Juvenile literature. 4. Denver Broncos (Football team) — Juvenile literature. [1. Elway, John, 1960-   . 2. Football players.] I. Title. II. Series.
GV939.E48F69 1990
92 — dc20
[796.332'092]
   [B]   89-28465
                                                 CIP
                                                  AC

Printed in the United States of America

10 9 8 7 6 5

Illustration Credits
Denver Broncos: pp. 6, 52; Croke/Visual Images: pp. 22, 24, 49; Tim Davis: pp. 15, 37, 40; Photography by Rod Hanna: pp. 9, 11, 20, 27, 29, 31, 42, 46, 55, 58; David Madison: pp. 16, 35.

Cover Photo: Photography by Rod Hanna

Contents

To the memory of
Walter Spearman, who inspired so many of us

Acknowledgments

To Jim Packett, of the Eastham (MA) Elementary School, for his editorial assistance. To Jim Saccomano of the Denver Broncos with special thanks. Also to Jim Greenidge of the New England Patriots, the Stanford University Sports Information department, and Pete Abitante of the National Football League.

— *Sports Great Books* —

Sports Great Roger Clemens
ISBN 0-89490-284-9

Sports Great John Elway
ISBN 0-89490-282-2

Sports Great Bo Jackson
ISBN 0-89490-281-4

Sports Great Magic Johnson
ISBN 0-89490-160-5

Sports Great Darryl Strawberry
ISBN 0-89490-291-1

Sports Great Herschel Walker
ISBN 0-89490-207-5

Chapter 1

In the career of every outstanding performer, there is usually a moment when the world suddenly realizes: here is a superstar. For a movie star, it can be winning an Oscar, or simply creating a memorable role. The same is true for an athlete. It can be winning a championship . . . or merely a major achievement that proves what all have been predicting — yes, this is a star.

For John Elway, three-time Super Bowl quarterback of the National Football League's Denver Broncos, that magic moment took place on a freezing January day in 1987. The setting was Cleveland, Ohio. The wind whipping in off Lake Erie created a wind-chill factor of only five degrees Farenheit for the bundled crowd of almost 80,000 in Cleveland Stadium.

The 1986 NFL campaign was racing to its climax. Today was the playoff game for the American Football Conference championship. To the winner would go an invitation to play in the Super Bowl with a chance for both gold and glory.

The Cleveland Browns' quarterback, Bernie Kosar, was regarded as one of the brightest talents in the National

Football League. But in John Elway, the Broncos had a quarterback who had been marked for greatness from his days as an all-American at Stanford University. In 1983, he had been the very first player chosen in the NFL college draft. He already had led the Broncos to a winning record in each of his four seasons. Three of those years his team had qualified for the playoffs.

John Elway shows off his scrambling ability.

Still, however, there were doubters. American sports fans tend to measure success only by who is Number One. Most athletes go through their entire careers without ever getting a chance to compete in the Olympics or fight for a championship or even contend for a title. But still, thinking only of the Super Bowl, the fans asked, "When will John Elway get to the Big One?" On this frozen January 11, they hoped to get their answer.

The first half was a standoff. Cleveland scored first on a six-yard touchdown pass from Kosar to Herman Fontenot for a 7–0 first quarter lead. The Broncos, however, rallied to go in front on a 19-yard field goal by Rich Karlis and a one-yard touchdown plunge by Gerald Wilhite. The touchdown had been set up by a 34-yard run by Elway. But then Mark Moseley kicked a 29-yard field goal for Cleveland with twenty seconds remaining in the second period. This left the score deadlocked at halftime, 10–10.

After three quarters, the Broncos led, 13–10, on another Karlis field goal. But then Moseley matched that three-pointer with another field goal of his own, and Kosar put the Browns on top, 20–13, when he completed a 48-yard scoring strike to Brian Brennan. There were less than six minutes left to play.

To make matters worse, the Broncos did not handle the following Cleveland kickoff cleanly. Gene Lang, a substitute running back, finally fell on the loose ball at the two. The Broncos found themselves 98 yards and five minutes and forty-three seconds away from the end of their season.

For John Elway, however, this was the moment he had been trained for. He had faced situations just as grim in big games in high school and in college, and he had often rallied his team to victory. He knew he could do it again for even higher stakes. His teammates could read the confidence in his eyes as they huddled up in their own end zone. "Ninety-eight yards to the Super Bowl," receiver Mark Jackson remembers thinking, and he had no doubt that John Elway would get them there.

Just about every long scoring drive contains several critical plays. The first of these for Denver came on the fifth play after the kickoff. It was second-and-seven from the 15. Elway ran for 11 yards and a first down at the Denver 26. On the next two plays he passed, first a 22-yard strike to Steve Sewell and then a 12-yarder to Steve Watson. The Broncos now found themselves with a first down at the Cleveland 40.

The Browns would not give up. An Elway pass fell incomplete, and on the next play the Denver quarterback was sacked for an 8-yard loss. This put the Broncos in a third-and-eighteen situation. But Elway kept the drive alive by gaining the required yardage with a 20-yard strike to Mark Jackson. Two plays later Elway hit Sewell for 14 yards to put the ball on the Cleveland 14-yard line. The clock now showed less than a minute to play.

Again an Elway pass fell incomplete, and again the quarterback's running skill became a factor as he dashed 9 yards to the Cleveland five. The seconds ticked away. On third down, Elway faded to pass. He spotted Jackson in the end zone and bull's-eye! A touchdown! Only thirty-nine seconds remained in the fourth quarter when Rich Karlis kicked the extra point for a 20–20 tie.

The Browns still had one more chance, but they were unable to move the ball in the closing seconds and the game went into overtime. The Browns won the toss, and got the first chance to score in the sudden death extra period. The first team to score any points would win the game. But the Denver defense held. And, following the Cleveland punt, Elway completed passes of 22 and 28 yards to put Karlis in position to kick the winning 33-yard field goal. The scoreboard told

John Elway celebrates at the end of "The Drive" against Cleveland.

the story: 23–20, Denver. The Broncos were on their way to the Super Bowl!

The overtime and the winning kick were almost an anti-climax. It was "The Drive" that had everyone talking. "It was the best drive I've ever seen. He's the only quarterback I've ever seen who could have pulled it off," marvelled Craig Morton, who had been the Broncos' quarterback in their only previous Super Bowl appearance.

There might have been a tendency to dismiss Elway's clutch performance as a once-in-a-lifetime fluke. The history of sports is filled with such stories. But, in John's case, the football world knew that this was no accident. They knew this was the kind of performance that eventually would be considered commonplace for John Elway. They always knew he had the ability. This merely proved it.

"On that drive, John Elway did everything that an Elway is capable of doing," Miami Coach Don Shula said. The Dolphin coach was speaking for the rest of the football world.

In his first seven years as a professional, Elway three times took his team to the Super Bowl. The Broncos made the playoffs five times and had won four division titles. They never had a losing record, and for four straight years they had won ten or more games. All this was accomplished with a team that even Denver coaches admitted would be lucky to win half its games without John Elway at quarterback.

No quarterback has done better, and as he entered his fifth season he was rewarded with a new six-year contract worth more than $12 million. That made him the highest paid player in NFL history at the time.

What made John Albert Elway worth this kind of money? A computer asked to describe the perfect quarterback probably would come up with a mirror image of the handsome, blond athlete with the toothy grin that flashes

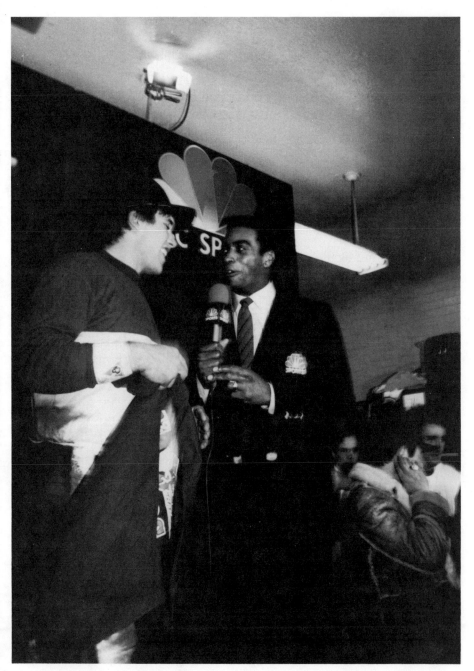

NBC's Ahmad Rashad interviews Elway after the Broncos beat the Browns for the chance to go to the Super Bowl.

confidence even in the most difficult situations. At six-foot, three-inches and 215 pounds, he is the ideal size for a quarterback. Nobody in football has a stronger arm. He can run, and he is by far the best scrambling passer in the league. He also has an uncanny knowledge of where his receivers are at all times.

In addition, John is intelligent and a competitor and, as Bronco Head Coach Dan Reeves sums up, "He's fun to watch and he's fun to coach and he has the kind of image that you like to see young people relate to. He's just a neat young guy."

In more technical terms, this is how Dan Reeves, himself a former college quarterback, evaluates John Elway:

"What does he do best?" Reeves considers the question. "Well, first of all, what he does best is win. That's key for any quarterback. And he probably performs at his best when things are toughest. The pressure does not bother him.

"The thing that he does," Reeves continues, "is put tremendous pressure on the defense. One, he does it with his scrambling because he's very hard to hem in. And, two, he has such a great arm that a receiver is never out of his range. So, put together, the defense is always trying to figure out how to contain him. That's got to be their first priority."

Getting down to more specifics and warming to his task, Reeves goes on without prompting. "He has tremendous vision of the field and I think that is one of the keys. A lot of quarterbacks run. I mean scramble to run. John really scrambles to buy more time to get his receivers open. He's always looking downfield to throw the ball and that means the defensive backs have to stay with their men and not come up to make the tackle or else he's going to kill 'em (with a pass).

"I think he can be the best ever because I've never seen a quarterback have all the ingredients that you need. He's got the temperament for it. He's got the competitiveness that you need. He's got the leadership. He's got all the physical qualities . . . and he's got more speed than any quarterback I've ever seen. He can really turn it on. I think it depends on how fast someone is chasing him . . . or if he has to run somebody down. Then he turns it up a notch."

Reeves admits he doesn't know how good Elway can be. Right now he rates him the equal of modern-day greats like Hall of Famers Roger Staubach and Terry Bradshaw "with the ability to get better."

But Reeves knows that a quarterback with John Elway's skill didn't just spring from nowhere off a college campus. "I bet he's thrown ten million passes since he was a kid," Dan Reeves says. "As a kid . . . " yes, that is when the John Elway story begins.

Chapter 2

John Elway had to work hard to be a great athlete, but you could say that he was born to be at least a good one. His grandfather played quarterback for a team in Pennsylvania. His mother played sports in high school. And his father was an outstanding athlete in high school. He played quarterback, too, so that makes John the third generation in his family to play the position.

John's father, Jack, was good enough to play sports in college. He's not very tall, but he was given a scholarship to play basketball as well as football at Washington State University. Injuries, however, prevented him from becoming a star. But sports had become part of his life, so he became a coach.

Today Mr. Elway doesn't look much like a former athlete. He even jokes about being short and kind of dumpy. Young John takes after his mother's side of the family when it comes to size. His mother is tall and so were her parents and grandparents. From his father, he got his burning desire to compete, and to win.

Young John Elway didn't have to wait very long to get his first coaching lesson from his dad. John was two years old when his father bought a plastic whiffle ball and bat set. They could play with it in the house and not worry about breaking anything. Dad prepared to pitch. John grabbed the bat.

John Elway is right-handed in everything he does. He took his first batting stance as a right-handed hitter because that was the way he had seen the other kids do it.

John's height comes from his mother's side of the family.

"No, no, no. That's not the way," Mr. Elway cried. He snatched the bat away from his son and made John turn around to stand up as a left-handed batter.

Left-handed hitters have a lot of technical advantages when it comes to playing baseball. One of them is stepping up to bat on the first base side of home plate. Starting out closer to the base by a stride or two can be very helpful if you're

Elway's dad was looking to his son's future when he taught John to bat left-handed.

trying to beat out an infield hit. Even then Jack Elway was looking ahead toward his son's sports future.

Today John says of the turn-around, "I never knew any other way to hit." Although he became famous as a football star, we will see later that John Elway's ability in baseball would play a major role in his sports career.

Batting left-handed wasn't the only basic sports lesson John learned at home. The entire Elway household was extremely competitive.

John has a twin sister and another sister who is eighteen months older. Even simple household chores were turned into a contest; a contest with winners and losers. Coach Elway would even time the kids taking out the garbage to see who could do it the fastest. When dad came home from a hard day at work, his three children would race to see who could get there first to bring him his newspaper.

When they were still in grade school, the twins shared a bedroom. They had bunkbeds, and John slept on top. Relatives recall that one night they had a race to see who could get into bed first. John lost. His two sisters had hidden the ladder to the top bunk.

Another time Mr. Elway was working around their house on the campus of the college where he was coaching, and he heard the loudspeaker down at the running track announce that "Elway" had just won a race in a kid's track meet. Mr. Elway couldn't understand why John didn't seem very happy when he got home that evening . . . until he found out that the winning Elway had been John's twin sister, Jana. Jana also grew up to be a pretty good athlete.

This competition also extended to report cards. It was a great feeling to bring home the best grades at the end of the term, and all three children were good students. This also paid off for John when it came time to choose a college. His grades were good enough so that he knew he would be accepted wherever he applied.

"To be successful, you've got to have that desire to win and that is something that has to be learned very early," Coach Elway says. His son agrees.

During this period when the children were growing up, there was another important lesson being taught in the Elway household. Mr. and Mrs. Elway did not insist that their children earn all A's in school, or that they be the greatest athletes in the neighborhood. "Whether it's playing sports, playing the piano, or going to school, all I ask is that you do your best," Mr. Elway told them.

"If we worked hard in class and the best we could get was a C, that was all right. But if we didn't work hard, even if we came home with a B, our parents would be angry because they knew we could have done better," John remembers.

Coach Elway worked very closely with his son in those early days. They would play with the whiffle ball set. John batted and his father pitched . . . and also broadcast an imaginary game. Even then, everything was made into a contest.

When John got to be a little older, his dad would gather all the baseballs in the house in a wash bucket. Then they would go out to a nearby park for some real batting practice. His dad pitched, and John hit. He never had enough. "One more bucket. One more bucket," he would plead.

His sisters, though, were not that enthusiastic because they had to chase baseballs all over the outfield. But their parents made it up to them with some girls-only skiing trips in the winter.

John remembers that the only time his dad ever spanked him was after one of these sessions in the park. College football coaches are very busy men, even the assistants. They work long hours. Jack Elway cherished the special time he could spend with his son, and he preferred that they work out alone. One day John surprised his dad by bringing along a few of his friends.

Mr. Elway made sure that the other boys got to bat first, and John didn't like that. When it finally was his turn, just before dark, he refused to bat. He sulked all the way home. "That's not the way to behave," his dad declared, and he gave his son a whack on the bottom.

As he was growing up, young John had trouble controlling his competitive nature. He wanted to win too badly. He would even yell at his teammates if he felt they weren't giving their best. But all it took was a look from his dad — the same look he remembered from that day at the playground — and John got his temper back under control.

The Elways also had a basketball hoop in the driveway, and father and son would play one-on-one before dinner. They quit this game, however, when John got big enough to start beating his dad. Coach Elway didn't like to lose, either.

It was during these early sessions that Coach Elway realized that his son could be something special as an athlete. He could see that John had good coordination. The only question was how big he would grow and how fast he would be able to run.

Coach Elway knew that no matter how many physical gifts John had inherited from his parents, they all would be wasted if he wasn't willing to work at it. Athletics at a high level is more than just a game. It requires a lot of hard work. "One more bucket. One more bucket." That was proof to Coach Elway that John was willing to pay at least part of the price.

Jack Elway also noticed that when it came time to work on different skills, John was willing to concentrate and learn.

This wasn't the fun part. The mechanics of hitting a baseball, for instance, can be very complicated. John listened — and asked questions — when his dad showed him what was involved in a major league swing. Throwing a football as a big-time quarterback also involves more than a game of catch in the back yard.

Even today as a Super Bowl quarterback, John Elway

Growing up, Elway would yell at his teammates if he thought they were slacking off.

remembers — and uses — the fundamentals he learned from his dad. These were the same fundamentals he practiced for hours on the football field and at every other opportunity. "He was always throwing something," old friends recall. Rocks, clods of dirt, snowballs; John was always the winner in a snowball fight. Later, when the Elways moved to southern California where it never snowed, John would pick lemons and oranges off the trees and toss them at targets. John is still embarrassed today when friends remind him that these often were moving targets — automobiles. Fortunately, nobody ever got hurt.

Once they realized that their son was willing and eager to work hard at sports, the Elways saw to it that he got a chance to succeed. No matter how tight the family budget, if John needed a new baseball glove or a pair of football shoes, they went out and bought him the best. If he had to get to a game or to practice for Little League baseball, Pop Warner League football, or YMCA League basketball, there always was somebody to take him there. One summer the family's brief vacation in the mountains was interrupted at least twice as his parents took turns driving John fifty miles each way to Little League baseball practice!

Because he was a football coach, Mr. Elway had less time to spend with his son during the autumn gridiron season. This meant that the football lessons had to be a little different. There were no long hours to spare for activities like baseball batting practice or basketball one-on-one.

However, as he got older, John was able to accompany his dad to practice. Sometimes he would even stay overnight in the players' dormitory. Later he would get to visit in the dressing room before and after workouts and even games.

When he was little, John would spend time at practice building "forts" out of the foam rubber blocking dummies. As he grew older, he became more aware of what was going on with the players. He saw just how hard these college athletes had to work to succeed. He saw how happy they were when they won; and how sad they felt then they lost.

This was when he promised himself that he would work as hard as he could to become a great athlete. That way, if he failed, he would never have to look back one day and say, "If only I had worked a little harder . . ."

Concentration is one of the fundamentals that helps Elway play well.

Chapter 3

If a coach wants to get ahead in his profession and make the Big Time, he has to be prepared to move from job to job and from city to city. He may have to join a new team to move up from assistant coach to head coach. He may have to move to advance from high school to the college level, or to the pros. He may go from a small college to one of the so-called major schools that appear every week on national television.

And always he understands that if his team doesn't win, he can be fired and forced to start the process all over again. That's true for assistant coaches, too, since they almost always are let go if the head man is replaced.

All this pressure to win does not make for a very secure life for the coach's family. Families in the armed forces move around a lot, too. They call the children "Army brats." "I was a 'coaching brat,' " John Elway says with a smile.

John remembers that some moves were more difficult than others. There was one move in particular when he was about twelve years old that really upset him. His dad, then an assistant coach, left the University of Montana in Missoula,

Montana, to join the staff at his old college, Washington State University in Pullman, Washington. The years when youngsters enter their teens are always difficult, even when the family isn't moving around. At Montana, John was just getting old enough to be a real part of his father's coaching life. "I'd hang on his shirt-tail wherever he went," John says.

Missoula also was where John first got involved in

Playing sports made it easier for John to make new friends in a new place.

organized sports. A "peewee" baseball league had been organized for young boys at the local playground, and John was one of the first to sign up. A year later he began YMCA basketball; then football.

Playing sports always made it easier for John to adapt to a new neighborhood and make new friends. As soon as the Elways moved into a new house, John would scout out the closest playground. "Every time you moved, you felt like an outsider," John recalls. "When you first get there you discover that all the friendships are already set up. Trying to make new friendships and being accepted by the other kids is one of the most difficult things there is."

John, however, did not mope at home watching television. He found the playground, and he hung around. "That way," he says, "when there was a game going on and they were a guy short, I was always there to be the extra guy to get in and play. It was just the persistence of standing around and watching a lot and when they needed that extra guy I was always the first one in line."

Needless to say, John Elway always established himself in a hurry as one of the best athletes in the neighborhood. It didn't take him long to go from being that "extra guy" to the first player chosen.

It got so he knew this would happen, too, and that also made the adjustment easier. "Being involved built your confidence. I had some success playing when I was young and therefore I had confidence that I wouldn't have any trouble blending in with the new kids," he says.

One of the toughest things John had to learn in those early years was controlling his temper. He had spent so much time around the competitive college athletes coached by his father that he thought everybody should be that serious. In baseball, he would throw his bat when he struck out. In basketball, it was much the same. He and his dad both remember vividly one particular YMCA league game when John totally lost his cool. He ended up raving and screaming at his teammates. It wasn't because they were losing, either. It was because John felt they were accepting their defeat and had stopped trying to win.

Mr. Elway seldom interfered in John's career once his boy started to receive formal coaching. But during this period he had to call him aside more than once. He pointed out that when John got so upset with his teammates it detracted from his own ability to perform. "You've got to be tough enough not to fall apart yourself," he told his son. On one occasion when John had thrown his bat after striking out he was reminded, "You get up there and take your licks, but you've got to be tough enough to take the bad with the good and continue to work hard."

John remains a tough loser and, as a quarterback, he knows there are times when he has to inspire his teammates to play harder. "He accepts the responsibility of being a quarterback," his dad says, "but at the same time he has compassion and patience with his teammates and he knows that the only thing he can really control is how he plays himself."

John's football career stalled briefly during the four years his dad coached at Washington State. He had played one year of Pop Warner League youth football in Missoula — as a running back. But there was no such program in Washington, so he concentrated on basketball and baseball. One summer he went to Washington State Coach George Raveling's basketball camp. Raveling, now head coach at Southern California, still kids him, "I told you to stick with basketball."

The big turning point for all the Elways came when John was about fifteen years old and finishing his freshman year in high school. The head coach at Washington State was fired, and Jack Elway thought he would be promoted to replace him. However, he was passed over for the job. And since this was his old college, the hurt was even greater. Because of this disappointment, he left Washington State, which is a member of the big-time Pacific Ten Conference, and took the job as

Sometimes a quarterback has to be a cheerleader.

head coach at California State College in Northridge, a suburb of Los Angeles. Cal State-Northridge wasn't "big time," but at least Jack Elway at last was a collegiate head coach.

John Elway by this time had made an emotional commitment to playing football. He continued to play basketball until he hurt his knee during the winter of his junior year in high school. And he stuck with baseball all through college for a change of pace in the spring. But football was his game, and he even gave up his favorite position, running back, because his dad wisely insisted he would have a better future throwing the ball.

"I guess Dad was right," John jokes now, but his freshman season as a quarterback in a Washington high school was not that rewarding. "All I did was hand off," he remembers unhappily.

All this changed with the move to southern California, where the sun always shined, and the weather always was mild. Some schools, in fact, worked at their football all year 'round.

By now, the entire Elway family was committed to helping John make it as a quarterback. Before Jack Elway even went looking for a new house, he scouted the area's high school coaches. Jack Neumeier, veteran coach at Granada Hills High School, was famous for teaching and using the passing game. So Jack Elway looked for a house in the Granada Hills school district. The house cost a lot more than he had been prepared to pay, but he swallowed hard and went ahead. That house was an investment — and it paid off.

Jack Neumeier had been thinking about retirement at the time. But when he realized what a gem had dropped into his lap, he put those plans on hold for a while. No coach ever turns his back on a potential Hall of Famer.

When John showed up at Granada Hills as a tenth grader,

Playing football year-round in sunny California helped Elway polish his skills.

the coaches all knew that he would be a great player for them. But the Granada Hills passing game was very complicated, and John had to start off on the junior varsity team while he learned the offense. Before the season was halfway over, however, he had been promoted to start for the varsity. Neumeier received some criticism for this decision, but, before long, everyone agreed he had made a wise move.

Elway led Granada Hills to the semifinals of the Los Angeles city playoffs. He passed for over 3,000 yards as a junior and had already passed for nineteen touchdowns and almost 2,000 yards when he hurt his knee in the sixth game of his senior year. That injury ended Elway's high school football career, but he already had showed enough ability to be rated one of the top high school quarterbacks in the nation.

As one of his coaches said, "John was the most tenacious competitor I ever worked with." And John managed to come back from his knee injury to lead Granada Hills to the city baseball championship. He even was named Los Angeles city high school Player of the Year as he compiled a .491 batting average.

Former Granada Hills teammates still remember some of John's special drills for improving his accuracy in passing the football. From thirty-five yards away, he would fire the ball at one of the goal posts, hitting it time and again, clang, clang, clang. Or he would have a teammate stand forty yards away and throw one football straight up in the air as high as he could. Elway then would throw another ball and hit the first one in midflight.

Still, John and his dad always felt that the best passing workouts were done with a live receiver. In a sports-minded community, there always was somebody to work out with, and the weather almost always was perfect. Even more helpful to Elway and the other Granada Hills players, Jack Neumeier

Elway's ability to fire the ball comes from the special drills he used to do in high school.

was able to organize summer "passing leagues" as part of the town recreation program. This enabled John and his teammates to polish their skills under competitive conditions.

There was one other advantage to growing up in Granada Hills. The Dallas Cowboys of the National Football League, always Elway's favorite, held their summer training camp each year at Thousand Oaks, California, only about forty-five minutes away by car. The Cowboys always welcomed visiting college coaches, and Jack Elway often showed up with his son. John collected all sorts of Cowboy souvenirs and got to see, in person, some of his heroes like Calvin Hill and Bob Hayes, the former Olympic sprinter. In fact, when he still had dreams of being a running back, John had chosen to wear Calvin Hill's jersey number 35.

Jack Elway once had worked as a part time scout for the Cowboys at Washington State. During one of his visits to Thousand Oaks, he may have asked personnel chief Gil Brandt if he still had the report the proud father had written up on his son several years earlier as a joke.

As Jack Elway tells it, he wrote down of his then twelve-year-old boy: "Great arm, speed, 6-2, 185 pounds, outstanding student, knows the game." By the time John was ready for the pros, he was 6-3, 204 pounds. His dad was just about on the nose in every aspect of the scouting report except for his notation that John had "a bad attitude."

His dad explains: "He wasn't taking out the garbage at the time." Sometimes he changes the punch line a bit to "failure to clean the swimming pool." But it's still a good story.

Chapter 4

John Elway was faced with some major decisions during his years at Granada Hills High School. The first choice was easy, selecting football over his other sports. He gave up basketball because it was too hard on his knees. And even though he continued in baseball, he never pitched full time because he wanted to save his powerful arm for throwing passes.

His choice of a lifestyle was more serious. There weren't any "Just Say No" anti-drug or anti-drinking programs in those days, and John remembers very vividly the peer pressure to be "one of the gang."

"Drugs and drinking were a big thing in high school and a lot of the guys were doing this and doing that and there was always a lot of pressure to do that, too," Elway says. "But I always felt that I was a better person than someone doing drugs and I never wanted to be lowered to their level. Even though they were my friends, I didn't respect the people that did that sort of thing.

"I didn't want to get caught in that. I wanted to be known as a straight arrow. That was something I was proud of, and I think if more kids took pride in being that way we wouldn't have all the problems that we've got now."

As he finished high school, John Elway's next decision was where to go to college. Because his grades were as high as his football standing, he had his choice of any school in the nation. Just about every college with a football program tried to recruit him. Academics were very important to John, but he also wanted to play professional football eventually. Therefore the college he chose would have to field a bigtime team and play a bigtime schedule.

John always had dreamed of playing in the Pacific Ten Conference, which includes outstanding universities in the Far West. John quickly zeroed in on Stanford University in Palo Alto, California, not far from San Francisco.

Stanford was competitive in Pac–10 football and boasted a long history of producing outstanding quarterbacks. The school, located on a beautiful campus, fielded strong teams in all sports, including baseball. And its academic standing was beyond compare. "I knew I would have the opportunity to be the best quarterback I could be at Stanford, but I also knew that if football didn't work out, I would always have a great education to fall back on," says Elway, who earned his Stanford degree in economics.

There was one problem. While John was graduating from high school, his dad also was graduating in his profession. Jack Elway moved up to become head coach at San Jose State, and this created a dilemma for young John. San Jose State represented a major step upward from Cal State-Northridge. But even though it was only twenty miles away from Stanford—and the two schools played each other every year—its level of competition was significantly lower.

John always had wanted to play football for his dad. And he knew, without being boastful, that he was a good enough player to make a real difference for his dad's team should he choose to enroll at San Jose State. Finally, he told his father, "If you really want me to go to San Jose with you, I will."

Coach Elway appreciated the offer. But, even though he likes to joke that "I had the best high school quarterback in America sitting across the breakfast table every morning and he still ended up playing against me," he knew that Stanford would be the best choice for his son.

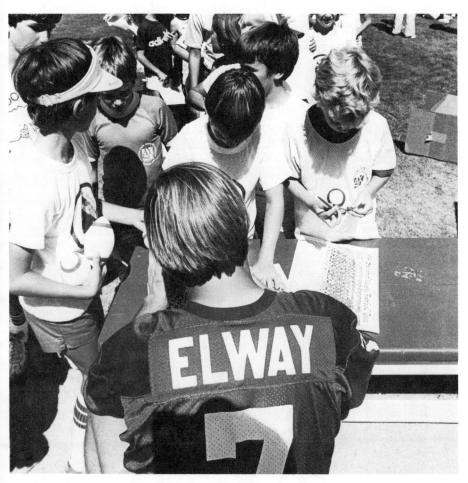

Even in college, Elway drew a crowd. Here he is at Stanford University Family Day in 1981.

Ironically, four years later, when John had just finished at Stanford, his dad was named head coach at that school. John, as a loyal Stanford alumnus—and dutiful son—finally was able to help by recruiting for Stanford.

Elway's college football career was an outstanding personal success. But although he established whole pages of passing records, there were difficult times as well.

Foremost among these were the games Stanford played against his father's team. Much was made of these meetings in the press, and John's mother and sisters always had to struggle with divided loyalties. Both John and his dad were relieved when the series was over. Each had won twice in the four years, but some of John's worst games at Stanford were recorded against San Jose State.

John was a standout from the day he showed up on campus. He threw the ball so hard, receivers had to worry about getting their fingers broken. After workouts, they showed off what came to be known as "The Elway Cross," a bruise on their chest where the nose of a jet-propelled football had left its mark.

John split the quarterback job with a returning senior his first year, and then took over by himself as he made all-America his sophomore season. Unfortunately, the Stanford team wasn't as gifted as its quarterback. The Stanford Cardinal won five, lost five, and tied one John's freshman season and then produced a 6–5 record his sophomore year. This was the high point. Even though Elway set five national and seventeen conference passing records, Stanford posted losing records John's last two years.

John's last college game was typical. Stanford went into its traditional closing game against archrival California with a 5–5 record. If they won, they would be invited to play in a postseason bowl game, the first in Elway's college career.

Elway beams the joy of victory after Stanford upsets top-ranked Washington in his senior year.

With less than a minute to go, Stanford had the ball deep in its own territory while trailing California, 19–17. Climaxing one of his greatest games, Elway drove his team downfield. At one point it was fourth down and 17 yards to go on the Stanford 13, and Elway rifled a bullet for a 30-yard completion to keep the drive going.

With four seconds to go, Elway had brought Stanford close enough to kick a 35-yard field goal that put the Cardinal in front, 20–19. Stanford players went crazy. So did their fans. The whole stadium was in a frenzy. Unfortunately, the Stanford band also forgot itself and streamed out on the field to serenade the apparent victory.

However, because four seconds remained on the clock, Stanford still had to kick off. The officials did not wait until the field was cleared. The teams were not even lined up properly when Stanford kicked off. Knowing this would be their last chance, California players forgot all caution and lateralled the ball wildly from man to man as they were about to be tackled. There were five laterals in all before the final California ball carrier barreled through the Stanford band—scattering tuba players like bowling pins—for the winning touchdown as the game ended. It was one of the zaniest plays in college football history.

The final score was 25–20, California. Elway's heroic effort was forgotten. There would be no bowl bid to cap his college career.

During his early days at Stanford, John continued to play varsity baseball. Although Elway had been clocked throwing a baseball more than ninety miles an hour as a high school junior, which is better than many major leaguers, he continued to avoid the pitcher's mound. Maybe he just wanted to protect his valuable arm. But some people think John preferred right field because he was tired of the spotlight that follows all football quarterbacks. It would be more of the same if he was a pitcher. He could relax and enjoy the game as an outfielder and let others do the interviews.

Elway hit only .269 with a single home run as a freshman and wondered if there was any point in continuing. However, his coach pointed out that many previous Stanford players had graduated to successful professional careers after doing not even that well as freshmen. Also, Elway was dividing his time between baseball and spring football practice, while many of the other baseball players were competing in their one sport all year 'round. The next year, Elway improved his college average to .361, and he cracked nine home runs. He continued to work out with the football team during the spring and often had to race from one field to the other and change uniforms with only minutes to spare.

At the end of Elway's sophomore season, the Stanford baseball team had to go out of town to compete in the conference playoffs.The football team had five more practice sessions left. John could not desert his baseball teammates at this point, and the football practices could not be postponed. So they were cancelled. Elway was so important to the football team that there was no point in practicing without him.

Elway's college baseball career lasted only two seasons. College rules allow an athlete to play professionally in one sport while remaining an amateur in any others. So the New York Yankees signed Elway to a contract worth $140,000 to play one summer season of minor league baseball. He then could go back to Stanford, complete his college football eligibility, and decide between the two sports. If he chose baseball, it would be with the Yankees.

Elway spent six weeks playing for Oneonta, New York, of the Single-A New York-Pennsylvania League. That's the low minor leagues, but still pretty tough competition for a football player coming in at mid-season. John started off poorly with only one hit in his first nineteen times at bat. However, eventually he hit .318 with twenty-five runs batted in (RBI). From his right field position he also threw out nine baserunners in forty-two games. The Oneonta Yankees were in first place when Elway left to return to school.

The scouting reports about his baseball talent were good. All who saw him were impressed with his athletic ability, his enthusiasm, his leadership — and his arm. All projected him as a future major leaguer, although they agreed he would have to spend several years in the minors.

All in all, it was a good summer's work. Most importantly, John had proved he could play baseball for a living. It would help his bargaining position to know there was something else he could do besides play football when the time came to choose a career.

Football practices were cancelled when John had to compete in conference baseball playoffs.

Chapter 5

Armed with his baseball alternative, John Elway was in the driver's seat at the conclusion of his college football career. The National Football League was gearing up for the 1983 annual player draft in which the teams with the worst records the previous year get the first choice of talent coming out of college. The system was created to even up the competition.

The class of 1983 was loaded with good quarterbacks. Six of them eventually would be chosen in the first round. But there was no question of who would be Number One. John Elway's name was at the top of every pro team's scouting report. He was big, he was strong, he could run well enough to scramble out of trouble, he was intelligent, and he had the strongest throwing arm to come out of college football in the last ten years.

The Denver Broncos, who picked fourth since they had recorded the fourth worst record in the league the previous year, wanted Elway badly. However, they knew he would be long gone by the time they got a chance to make their pick.

The first choice in the draft belonged to the Baltimore

The Denver Broncos put quarterback John Elway at the top of their list at the NFL college draft.

Colts, who at that time had not yet moved to Indianapolis. Under normal circumstances, their choice of Elway would have been automatic. Most players coming out of college just shrug their shoulders and go where they're drafted even if they hate the town and the team. But Elway was not a normal case. Before the draft, he announced that he preferred to play his professional football on the West Coast. When questioned by the Colts to clarify his intentions, he said, in effect, that he especially meant he would never play in Baltimore. He then hung up on the Baltimore coach after warning him not to waste a draft pick. (Later Elway would explain that he really had nothing against the city of Baltimore. He simply did not like their coach — who eventually lost his position — or the way the franchise was operated.)

Elway's warning did not impress the Colts, however. They went ahead and made the Stanford quarterback their leadoff pick. The Los Angeles Rams followed up by choosing running back Eric Dickerson of Southern Methodist University. Seattle chose runningback Curt Warner of Penn State, and Denver completed the first four by selecting offensive lineman Chris Hinton of Northwestern. What followed was as Elway had warned. He refused to sign a contract with Baltimore. As weeks passed, Colts owner Robert Irsay became more and more nervous about ending up with nothing to show for the first choice in the entire draft.

Meanwhile, the Broncos had some inside information. The day of the draft, Baltimore Coach Frank Kush had called Coach Dan Reeves of Denver. They discussed the player each was going to pick. During the conversation, Kush hinted that he kind of liked the player the Broncos expected to take, Chris Hinton.

As the Elway holdout continued, the Broncos began to discuss the situation among themselves. Reeves recalled the past conversation with Baltimore's coach. "I know we've got a player they'd like to have," Reeves told his owner, referring to Hinton.That was all the owner, Edgar Kaiser, had to hear. He knew the Colts' owner, called him up, and the deal was made: John Elway — or at least the rights to John Elway since he hadn't yet signed — was traded from Baltimore to Denver in exchange for Chris Hinton and the Broncos' first choice in the 1984 college draft. Mark Herrmann, an experienced substitute quarterback, also was sent to the Colts in the trade.

Fans in Denver were overjoyed. Baltimore was stunned. John Elway continued to use his baseball option as leverage in contract talks, but in the end — as almost everyone expected — he signed with football for a five-year $5 million contract. This made him the highest-paid player in the league before he had played a down.

If John Elway thought he could just quietly show up in Denver to learn his new trade as an NFL quarterback, he was mistaken. Because of his notoriety as the Number One draft pick in the entire league, the staggering numbers in his contract, the controversy surrounding his refusal to sign with Baltimore, and his use of the baseball alternative to get a better deal, John Elway had become famous.

To make matters worse, Denver's two newspapers were engaged in a hot battle for readers, and John Elway was the biggest story to hit town in years. The two papers tried to outdo each other in covering the new quarterback. Each ran a daily Elway Watch column that chronicled his every move from when he got a haircut to what he ordered for breakfast. The pressure was unbearable.

Thanks in large measure to the football training he had absorbed tagging along behind his father, and the passing offense he had been exposed to in high school and college, John was a quick learner. He did well in the four pre-season exhibition games, and Coach Reeves bowed to public pressure by naming the rookie to start the regular season.

Reeves today admits that this was a major mistake. Most pro football teams use the exhibition season to evaluate talent. They employ simple defenses. They do not put in their complicated, disguised combination alignments until the regular season has begun.

John Elway was not prepared for what he faced when he stepped under center for his first games of the official schedule. The Broncos won their first two decisions, but Elway suffered minor injuries in both starts, and veteran Steve DeBerg had to come to his rescue on both occasions. Elway's next three starts were disastrous losses. He was totally befuddled. In one game he even lined up behind one of the guards instead of the center to everyone's embarrassment. "Wrong guy! Wrong guy!" the guard kept yelling until Elway realized his error.

Elway calls that moment the lowest point of his entire athletic career. Commentators asked out loud, "Is Elway a $5 Million Mistake?"

Coach Reeves knew he had to bench Elway before his prize rookie's confidence was totally shattered. Fierce competitor that he is, John still was able to greet his demotion with a sense of relief. Even though he had never been benched before at any level of play, he often had listened to his father agonizing over similar decisions. So he knew what Coach Reeves was thinking. Elway realized he needed a break to pull himself together.

Today, Dan Reeves is thankful that the decision to start Elway as a raw rookie did not ruin the quarterback for good. Such things have happened. Because quarterback is a leadership position, they must be handled very carefully. But

Elway was not prepared for what he faced in the first games of the regular season.

Reeves was a young coach, too, and he and Elway have done a lot of growing up together.

"John was like a student who had been studying Spanish in the classroom and passed all the written tests. Then, all of a sudden, he finds himself in the middle of Mexico and he can't understand a thing they're saying, it's all coming at him so fast," Reeves realizes now.

"I was not afforded the luxury of being a rookie," John says, looking back, and through the Broncos' next four games he did not get to play a down.

He stood on the sidelines, watched the action, and learned. Week by week his understanding of the pro game increased. A great cloud was lifted. For the fifth game of John's demotion, Steve DeBerg again was the starter, but the veteran got hurt. Elway had to come off the bench. But now he was ready. He started five of the Broncos' last six regular season games and did well enough for Denver to qualify for the playoffs for the first time in four years. They finished the season with a 9–7 record.

Although the veteran DeBerg started the Broncos' first-round playoff game, Elway saw considerable action in the 31–7 loss. DeBerg then was traded away in the off-season, and there was no question that when the 1984 season rolled around, John Elway would be Denver's Number One quarterback.

The difficult rookie season had served as a learning experience for Elway in more ways than simply discovering how to recognize professional defenses. John also became aware of how much of a commitment was involved and just what he would have to do to succeed as a professional. His awesome natural ability no longer would be enough.

Following the season, John married his college sweetheart — a former varsity swimming star at Stanford — and he and Janet (who now have two daughters and a son) moved to Denver year 'round. That way they hoped to become more a part of the community. From a football standpoint, Elway now would be living only a short drive from the Broncos' training complex. He and Coach Reeves could study films together, and there would be more incentive to work out on a regular basis.

Because he had always been "in season" in one sport or another, John never needed to work out to keep in shape. He really saw no need to lift weights, either. He was a quarterback. Quarterbacks never beat up on people.

Coach Reeves knew, however, that as a running quarterback, Elway did indeed need some more muscle if he was going to survive in the National Football League. He worried about the best way to approach his young star about this. After all, John had come pretty far without the use of any barbells.

The answer came from Reeves' past as a player with the Dallas Cowboys. Roger Staubach and Reeves had been teammates when the Cowboys were winning one championship after another. Staubach, like Elway, had been a scrambling quarterback, good enough at running and passing to be honored with election to the Pro Football Hall of Fame. One day early in the off-season, Roger Staubach called John Elway on the phone. Of course, Reeves had asked him to do it. But Staubach was sincere when he lectured Elway on the importance of lifting weights.

It was not surprising that the lecture was effective. "Staubach was my childhood idol," John confessed. And so, before many days, Elway had reported to the weight room to start a program specially designed for him. While there, he was introduced to a new Bronco assistant coach named Mike

Shanahan, who had just been hired to take charge of Denver's offense.

Shanahan was young enough so that he and Elway could work out together. Six days a week—one more than the rest of the quarterbacks—for two and a half hours a day, Elway worked out with Coach Shanahan. These workouts lasted for three months.

In July, when the time for training camp arrived, John Elway's emotional scars from that disastrous rookie season had healed. And his body revealed a new physical toughness. Ten pounds of muscle had been added. A newly mature and muscled John Elway was ready to tackle the National Football League.

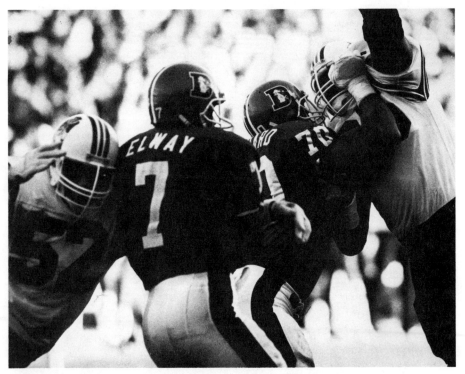

Beefing up his muscles helped Elway survive some crushing plays in the NFL.

Chapter 6

It may have been an exhibition game, Mike Shanahan recalls. John Elway was scrambling to his left from the opponents' 35-yard-line. Suddenly, he stopped and, still off balance, he threw a bullet pass to receiver Butch Johnson, who had just slipped free for an instant.

Let Shanahan describe it. "It was a bullet, travelled about 40 yards and never more than 10 feet off the ground. He threw it between two defenders for a touchdown. I remember saying, 'Boy, they never did that at Eastern Illinois,' which is where I had just come from."

It was on this play early in the 1984 season that Mike Shanahan, the rookie assistant coach, realized he had something special in John Elway.

That play displayed every aspect of Elway's talents: it showed how he could scramble out of trouble, it showed off the strength of his arm, and it illustrated his ability to keep the whole field in view even as he was scrambling. Also, it pointed out that he knew where every receiver was going to be — and demonstrated his confidence in his ability to complete a pass no matter how good the coverage.

Mike Shanahan could not have made a wiser judgment. John Elway was, indeed, ready to shine in the National Football League. Except for two games when he was injured, he started every game for the Denver Broncos as he began a five-year streak during which he would lead his team to four playoff appearances and more victories than any other quarterback in the league.

Starting with a 20–17 victory over Cincinnati, John led the Broncos to a 13–3 record for 1984 and first place in the American Football Conference's Western Division. This was the most victories in the history of the Denver franchise, which was founded in 1960, and the Broncos' first division championship since 1978.

Winning the title put Denver in the playoffs against Pittsburgh. They played before the usual sellout crowd of more than 76,000 screaming Orange-clad Denver fans in their Mile High Stadium. The Broncos scored first, and they led again in the third period. But, although Elway passed for two touchdowns, the Steelers won, 24–17.

The finish was disappointing, but the season gave cause for great optimism. The team was improving, and John Elway was fulfilling his potential.

Potential. Little did John realize how that word would grow to haunt him. In the words of the Denver Bronco press guide, in 1985 "Elway took some spectacular steps forward… " He set one record after another, he avoided injury, and he led the Broncos to an 11–5 record.

That record, however, was not good enough to win the division championship as the Los Angeles Raiders finished with twelve victories and only four losses. Because of the NFL's complicated system of tie-breakers, the Broncos weren't even able to qualify for the playoffs with a special "wild card" invitation, even though two teams in their rival National Football Conference did make it with fewer victories.

Nobody could fault Elway for the Broncos' failure to make the playoffs. But in pro football, the quarterback always gets most of the praise when the team wins — and most of the blame when it loses.

Taking a few "spectacular steps foward," Elway dives for key yardage.

The favorite question around Denver that off-season was, "When is John Elway going to live up to his potential?" The answer would not be long in coming as the Broncos shot out of the gate in 1986 by winning their first six games and eight of their first nine. Elway was playing with winning confidence.

The Broncos lost four of their last seven games, but their fans blamed this slump on a natural letdown following an outstanding start. Despite their poor finish, the Broncos won the AFC's Western Division title for the second time in three years.They opened the 1986 playoffs at home against the New England Patriots.

The game was a classic thriller as these two long-time rivals took turns holding the lead. It was Denver, 3–0; then New England, 7–3; Denver, 10–7 on a 22-yard run by Elway; then New England, 17–13.

That's the way it stood when Elway connected with wide receiver Vance Johnson for a 48-yard touchdown pass on the last play of the third period. That score gave Denver a 20–17 lead, and the Broncos held on for their first playoff victory in nine seasons, 22–17.

This victory set the stage for the Broncos to move on to Cleveland for the thrilling 23–20 overtime victory over the Browns climaxed by "The Drive" that will live forever in Denver memory. A conference championship means a lot, but its real significance is that it qualifies the winner to compete in the Super Bowl. This game, given special emphasis because it is designated by Roman numerals, is the most highly publicized team athletic contest in sports.

The Broncos had played in Super Bowl XII following the 1977 season and lost to the Dallas Cowboys, 27–10. Now it was time for Super Bowl XXI. This game was to be played in the Rose Bowl stadium in Pasadena, California, just outside

Los Angeles and not far from John Elway's home town. Denver's opponent would be the National Football Conference champion New York Giants.

The Giants had beaten the Broncos, 19–16, during Denver's slump late in the season, but they had come away with tremendous respect for Elway. "He was one quarterback we didn't want to see again," Giant defensive tackle Jim Burt said. Football experts agreed that against the Giants' powerful defense, "You have to give Denver a chance to win for one reason only: John Elway."

John lived up to all those expectations early in the game. The Broncos moved with the opening kickoff in range for a Rich Karlis field goal of 48 yards and a 3–0 lead. After the Giants drove right back to go on top, 7–3, Elway again took command. He led his team on a scoring drive that was completed when John ran the ball into the end zone from four yards out for a 10–7 advantage.

This would mark the high point of Denver's Super Bowl. Although the Broncos continued to dominate the first half, they missed on two field goal attempts and got the worst of a controversial call by the officials. An Elway pass that would have gotten Denver out of deep trouble was ruled incomplete as Bronco fans booed loud and long.

This play was critical because on the very next down, defensive end George Martin of the Giants broke through to tackle Elway in the end zone for a safety, which gave the Giants two points and cut Denver's lead to one. With Elway running and passing for 200 of his team's 201 yards in total offense, the Broncos had been presented with an opportunity to build up a pretty good cushion in the first half. Instead, they were able to go off the field at halftime with only a 10–9 margin.

From here, the Giants took charge. Scoring seventeen

points in the third period alone, they roared to a 33–10 lead. Elway achieved one last moment of hollow glory when he hit Vance Johnson for a 47-yard touchdown pass in the final period. But by then it was too late. The game ended in a 39–20 Denver loss.

Phil Simms, the Giants' quarterback, emerged as the game's Most Valuable Player, but nobody could blame John

Elway is under pressure from the Giants' pass rush in Super Bowl XXI.

Elway for Denver's one-sided defeat. "If they'd all played as well as John, we'd have won the game," said Denver Coach Dan Reeves.

The Super Bowl defeat left no lasting scars on Elway. The following week he passed for the game's only touchdown in his first appearance in the NFL's annual all-star game, the Pro Bowl.

The 1987 season was marked by a players' strike that saw makeshift teams play part of the season. But the Bronco regulars regrouped when the strike ended and won six of their last seven games. Their 10–4–1 record—the best in the AFC—was good for a second straight division title.

The Broncos walloped Houston in their first playoff game, 34–10, as Elway passed for two touchdowns and ran for a third. Then, once again, the Cleveland Browns stood between Denver and the Super Bowl.

This time the game for the AFC championship was played in Denver, and once again it was loaded with drama. The Broncos took leads of 14–0 in the first quarter and 21–3 at the half, but the Browns tied the score at 31–31 in the fourth quarter.

As if in an instant replay from the previous year, Elway once more had to lead Denver on a long scoring drive with the clock winding down. Starting on their own 25, the Broncos moved downfield until Elway collaborated with running back Sammy Winder on a 20-yard touchdown pass with four minutes to go.

The Denver defense was gasping for air when the Browns got the ball back. The Broncos' lead was in danger as Cleveland moved downfield. But then Denver's Jeremiah Castile recovered a Cleveland fumble at the Bronco three to assure the 38–33 victory and a return trip to the Super Bowl.

Super Bowl XXII was played in San Diego, California,

also not far from John Elway's old back yard, and the Broncos' opponent this time was the Washington Redskins. Again Denver started strong. The Broncos jumped out to a 10–0 first-quarter lead on a 56-yard pass from Elway to Ricky Nattiel on their first play from scrimmage and a 24-yard Rich Karlis field goal.

But this year the Broncos began to unravel even sooner than they had in Super Bowl XXI. The Redskins exploded for thirty-five points in the second period and coasted home for a 42–10 victory. Even Elway had his problems. He was intercepted three times and sacked five times. Once again his opposing quarterback — this time the relatively unsung Doug Williams — was named the game's Most Valuable Player.

The rest of the football world recognized Elway's importance to his team when he was named the NFL's Most Valuable Player by the Associated Press and the American Football Conference Most Valuable Player by United Press International and the Football News. And the Broncos rewarded him with his record $12 million contract before the 1988 season.

The season of 1988 matched his rookie campaign as the most troubled of Elway's career. The assistant coach who had played such a vital role in his success, Mike Shanahan, left the team to become head coach of the Los Angeles Raiders. John's father was not retained as head coach at Stanford. And John suffered through a variety of injuries.

A bad ankle that limited his mobility kept Elway on the sidelines for two games, and he suffered an elbow injury on his throwing arm that required off-season surgery. Still, John kept the Broncos in playoff contention until the final week of the season when they won their last game for an 8–8 record. He passed as best he could despite the ailing elbow. He ran as best he could with the sore ankle that had to be heavily taped

John Elway and Head Coach Dan Reeves confer on the sidelines.

before every game. And, in a desperate innovation tried by Coach Dan Reeves to upset the opposition, John even punted occasionally in a surprise move when he lined up deep in the so-called shotgun or passing formation.

None of it really worked, but through it all John Elway retained the respect of his coaches, the fans and, above all, his teammates. In one of Denver's final games, the television cameras panned down to show the tape wrapping the ankles of his various receivers. There, printed in black ink for all to see were the words: MR. ELWAY.

It was a quiet notice that, despite their troubles, the Broncos all knew that if they were to get back to the playoffs — and win that elusive Super Bowl crown — it would be Mr. Elway, John Elway, taking them there.

And he did. The Denver Broncos had a lot to feel good about as they began the 1989 season.

John Elway was healthy after undergoing surgery on his right elbow, his passing arm. The defense had a new coach, Wade Phillips. The offense gained a new dimension when Bobby Humphrey was drafted from Alabama.

Humphrey, a swift and dangerous halfback, quickly emerged as the Broncos' first real running threat in years. He ran for 1,000 yards his rookie season and was named the team's most valuable player. He took a lot of the pressure off quarterback Elway.

For the first time, John Elway didn't have to worry about doing it all himself. As the season progressed, he even got a little extra help. Mike Shanahan, his old quarterback coach, was let go in the middle of the season with the Los Angeles Raiders after six games. He immediately was rehired by the Broncos and reunited with Elway. The Broncos started quickly, winning their first three games before heading to Cleveland.

This time, John Elway's 7-yard touchdown pass to Vance Johnson created a 13–13 tie with just under four minutes to play. But Matt Bahr of Cleveland kicked a 48-yard field goal to win for the Browns, 16–13, as time ran out at the end ofthe game.

The Broncos, however, scarcely missed a beat. They won seven of their next eight games, including a 14–10 victory over Washington without Elway. He was downed by a stomach virus.

A week later the Broncos clinched their fourth division championship of the 1980s with a 41–14 victory over Seattle. Then the Broncos suffered through a slump at the end of regular season play.

They lost three of their last four games. Elway played a full month while handicapped by the pain from a cracked rib. The Broncos barely made it past their first Super Bowl playoff opponent, the Pittsburgh Steelers.

Then they came from behind with less than two and a half minutes left to beat Pittsburgh, 24–23. For the third time in four years the road to the Super Bowl was blocked by Cleveland.

But Elway led the Broncos to victory, to the delight of the sellout crowd at Mile High Stadium. He completed touchdown passes of seventy, thirty-nine, and five yards and was not intercepted once. He led all rushers by gaining thirty-nine yards on five carries in the 37–21 runaway.

Denver then prepared to meet the defending champion San Francisco 49ers in Super Bowl XXIV in New Orleans two weeks later. If there was a cloud, it was the cracked ribs suffered by rookie running sensation Bobby Humphrey against the Cleveland Browns. Humphrey was able to start against the 49ers, but his damaging fumble in the first period opened the floodgates for another lopsided Denver defeat.

The 49ers scored first for a 7–0 lead. The Broncos retaliated with a field goal. They were driving for another score when San Francisco recovered Humphrey's fumble near midfield. Ten plays later, the 49ers scored again for a 13–3 lead. The rout was on.

When the final gun sounded, the Broncos had lost, 55–10. It was the most one-sided loss in Super Bowl history. By failing for the fourth time, the Broncos tied a National Football League record.

Dan Reeves, Denver's coach, had to put things in perspective for his team and for John Elway. "We're still the AFC champions," he declared. "Someone has to take that away from us."

For his quarterback, he noted confidently, "John is tough. He is tough enough to realize the way this game is learned . . . I know how competitive John is . . . and I think, personally, he'll be better from it and more determined than ever."

From 1990 to 1995 Elway was able to lead the Broncos into the playoffs only twice. The first time was in 1991, when the Broncos won their division, but were defeated by the Buffalo Bills in the AFC Championship Game, 10–7. In 1993, Elway had a career year. He led the league in attempts (551), completions (348), and yards passing (4,030), and once again the Broncos made the playoffs. This time they lost a Wildcard game to the Los Angeles Raiders, 42–24. After missing the playoffs in 1994 and 1995, Elway and the Broncos hope to return to championship form in 1996.

Career Statistics

CAREER RECORD

YEAR	CLUB	PASS ATT.	PASS COMPL.	PASS YARDS	TOUCH-DOWNS	INTER-CEPTS
1979	Stanford	96	50	544	6	3
1980	Stanford	379	248	2,889	27	11
1981	Stanford	366	214	2,674	20	13
1982	Stanford	405	262	3,242	24	12
1983	Denver	259	123	1,663	7	14
1984	Denver	380	214	2,598	18	15
1985	Denver	605	327	3,891	22	23
1986	Denver	504	280	3,485	19	13
1987	Denver	410	224	3,198	19	12
1988	Denver	496	274	3,309	17	19
1989	Denver	416	223	3,051	18	18
1990	Denver	502	294	3,526	15	14
1991	Denver	451	242	3,253	13	12
1992	Denver	316	174	2,242	10	17
1993	Denver	551	348	4,030	25	10
1994	Denver	494	307	3,490	16	10
1995	Denver	542	316	3,970	26	14
NFL Totals		5,926	3,346	41,706	225	191

SUPER BOWL RECORD

YEAR	OPPONENT	PASS ATT.	PASS COMPL.	PASS YARDS	TOUCH-DOWNS	INTER-CEPTS
1987	Giants	37	22	304	1	
1988	Redskins	28	14	257	1	3
1989	49ers	26	10	108	0	2

Index

Morton, Craig, 10
Moseley, Mark, 7

N
National Football League
    (NFL), 41, 51, 61
Nattiel, Ricky, 57
Neumeier, Jack, 28, 30
New England Patriots, 53
New York Giants, 54-55
New York Yankees, 39

O
Oneonta Yankees, 39-40

P
Pacific Ten Conference, 27,
    34
Phillips, Wade, 59
Pittsburgh Steelers, 51, 60
Pro Bowl, 56

R
Raveling, George, 26
Reeves, Dan, 12-13, 43-45,
    47-48, 56, 59, 61

S
San Francisco 49ers, 60-61
San Jose State, 34-36
Seattle Seahawks, 43, 60
Sewell, Steve, 8
Shanahan, Mike, 48-51, 57,
    59
Shula, Don, 10
Simms, Phil, 55
Southern California
    University, 26
Stanford University, 6, 34,
    36, 38-39, 47, 57
Staubach, Roger, 13, 48

W
Warner, Curt, 43
Washington Redskins, 57, 60
Washington State University,
    24, 26-27, 32
Watson, Steve, 8
Wilhite, Gerald, 7
Williams, Doug, 57
Winder, Sammy, 56